THE VIRGIN BIRTH

THE VIRGIN BIRTH

BY
FREDERIC PALMER, D.D.
HARVARD UNIVERSITY

WIPF & STOCK · Eugene, Oregon

Wipf and Stock Publishers
199 W 8th Ave, Suite 3
Eugene, OR 97401

The Virgin Birth
By Palmer, Frederic
Softcover ISBN-13: 978-1-6667-6109-2
Hardcover ISBN-13: 978-1-6667-6110-8
eBook ISBN-13: 978-1-6667-6111-5
Publication date 10/4/2022
Previously published by The Macmillan Company, 1924

This edition is a scanned facsimile of the original edition published in 1924.

CONTENTS

CHAPTER		PAGE
I.	THE BIBLICAL EVIDENCE	1
II.	THE GROWTH OF THE DOCTRINE	17
III.	MIRACLES	32
IV.	THE VIRGIN BIRTH AND THE CREEDS	45

THE VIRGIN BIRTH

THE VIRGIN BIRTH

CHAPTER I

THE BIBLICAL EVIDENCE

Perhaps no part of the story of Jesus has appealed to the heart of humanity with a more tender touch than the gospel of the Infancy. The Mother and the Babe have been the centre of Christian art and have interpreted the reality of the Incarnation and the sacredness of all childhood. It may seem, at first, that any change in our view of the traditional facts must involve serious loss; that if the Virgin Birth should prove to be unhistorical, much of the preciousness of the gospel story would be gone.

In the face of such an apprehension, however, it is assuring to note how little the mode of Jesus' birth has, in fact, to do with the rest of the early history—Bethlehem and the manger, the angels, the Magi, the Temple. These are not affected but remain the same on any theory we may adopt as to the mode of his birth. And indeed if we may believe that his birth, like the rest of his life, was subject to the common conditions of humanity, there opens before us a larger and more comforting view of his person, a bond of closer intimacy with him, a means of salvation, more precious and potent than were possible before. Whatever conclusion, therefore, our investigation may reach, we need not fear that it will prove more meagre in spiritual sustenance or less enkindling for devotion.

Our earliest Gospel, that of St. Mark, dating probably about 70 A.D., makes no mention of the Virgin Birth. According to it "the beginning of the gospel of Jesus Christ the Son of God" was the preaching of John the Baptist.[1] In the middle of the second century we find the Virgin Birth fully established as a doctrine of the Christian Church, though apparently not long established; for Justin Martyr replies to the charge that it is an innovation by comparing it with similar ideas long prevalent in the heathen world as to the origin of the so-called sons of Zeus.[2] Between these two dates (70 A.D. and 150 A.D.) therefore, it seems to have gained recognition; though Justin declares there are still some Christians who do not hold it, of whom, however, he is not one. If we are wise, we shall not declare that the two passages of the Gospels in which alone it is mentioned settle the matter regardless

[1] St. Mark, 1, 1.
[2] Apol. 1, 21.

The Biblical Evidence

of other evidence, nor shall we attempt unscientifically to prove a negative and maintain that birth from a virgin is absolutely impossible. Instead, we shall weigh patiently the conflicting evidence in the New Testament and form our opinion according to its weight.

There are two different views of the birth of Jesus, each with difficulties of its own. The one —that he had no human father—is confronted by the strong presumption to a modern mind against the occurrence of such an event; moreover, taking the story as it stands, it must be explained why the first generation of Christians either did not know of it or maintained strict silence on the subject, so far as we are aware, until near the end of the first century, and then referred to it in only two passages of the Christian documents. The other view—that he had a human father, and that the belief in the Virgin Birth arose from exigencies in the thought of the time—has to meet the difficulty that historic evidence exhibiting the growth of such a belief is lacking.

Each of these two views finds support in the New Testament. The Virgin Birth is directly asserted in one passage and perhaps asserted or implied in another. There is no question that, according to most manuscript texts, it is directly asserted in St. Matt. 1,18-25:

The Virgin Birth

"Now the birth of Jesus Christ was on this wise: When as his mother Mary was espoused to Joseph, before they came together, she was found with child of the Holy Ghost. Then Joseph her husband, being a just man, and not willing to make her a public example, was minded to put her away privily. But while he thought on these things, behold, the angel of the Lord appeared unto him in a dream, saying, Joseph, thou son of David, fear not to take unto thee Mary thy wife; for that which is conceived in her is of the Holy Ghost. And she shall bring forth a son, and thou shalt call his name JESUS; for he shall save his people from their sins. Now all this was done, that it might be fulfilled which was spoken of the Lord by the prophet, saying, Behold, a virgin shall be with child, and shall bring forth a son, and they shall call his name Emmanuel, which being interpreted is, God with us. Then Joseph being raised from sleep did as the angel of the Lord had bidden him, and took unto him his wife; And knew her not till she had brought forth her first-born son; and he called his name JESUS."

The Sinai-Syriac MS., dating from the beginning of the fifth century, gives 1,16 as follows: "Joseph, to whom was betrothed Mary the virgin, begat Jesus, who is called the Christ"; and it adds to the Received Text in 1,21 two words, "she shall bear *to thee* a son," and again in 1,25, "she bore *to him* a son." The wording of the reference to Mary in this passage makes it plain that a belief in the Virgin Birth was already established at the time it was written, and established so firmly that its author could refer to her by her well-known title for identification, though, as he has just said, it was not actually descriptive of her state. In the passage quoted (Isa. 7,14), the Hebrew word here rendered "virgin" means

The Biblical Evidence

more accurately a marriageable young woman without regard to her condition. The passage is quoted by the author of the Gospel not as a prophecy of the Virgin Birth, but of the giving to the child Jesus a name expressive of his divine function. The Jews never regarded this passage in Isaiah as Messianic.

The second reference [3] is less clear. An angel announces to Mary that she shall become the mother of a child called Jesus. She questions this prediction in the absence of sexual intercourse, apparently assuming that it is expected to take place at once. But the angel answers, "The Holy Ghost shall come upon thee, and the power of the Highest shall overshadow thee; therefore also that holy thing which shall be born of thee shall be called a son of God." Nothing here directly excludes human paternity; and there are those who maintain it is consistent with such paternity on the ground that it might be said of any child, since every child is a child of God. It may be questioned, however, whether that is not a thought too modern for the occasion, one which would not be brought forward except to explain away a conclusion regarded as undesirable. It seems more probable that the author of these words considered them to imply a divine and not a human parentage.

These are the only passages in the New Testa-

[3] St. Luke 1, 26-36.

ment in which virgin birth is asserted or so much as hinted at. On the other hand, many passages assert or imply the opposite view. Mary, the person who should have known most about the matter, calls Joseph his father: "Thy father and I have sought thee sorrowing."[4] The explanation has been offered that she is here adopting the common usage of her Nazareth townspeople without reference to the actual fact. But there is no indication that such is the case, and it is difficult to believe that such an explanation would have been advanced except to buttress a pre-established theory. The author of the third Gospel, on whose careful research in regard to the story of the infancy much emphasis has been laid, apparently adopted Mary's view, for he calls Joseph and Mary the "parents" of Jesus;[5] and in one instance,[6] immediately after using "parents," he speaks of "Joseph and his mother," as if he regarded the two phrases as equivalent. This latter may, however, have been part of the growing movement in Christian circles to avoid speaking of Joseph as Jesus' father, before the substitution had become more thoroughgoing. The earlier texts show no objection to the use of "parents," while the later texts substitute other expressions. Thus while St. Luke 2,33 reads, in

[4] St. Luke 2, 48.
[5] *Ibid.* 27-41.
[6] *Ibid.* 43.

The Biblical Evidence

the earlier manuscript text: "his father and mother," the later manuscript text has "Joseph and his mother." [7]

The opinion of the community in regard to the paternity of Jesus is not conclusive but it must carry weight. He is held to be the son of Joseph, the well-known carpenter.[8] This view Jesus himself, according to the fourth Gospel, apparently endorses. For when his opponents object that he cannot be the Christ because they know his antecedents—his birth-place and parentage—whereas the Christ will appear no one knows from whence, he accepts their statements in regard to his antecedents as correct, but declares it to be no bar to his Messiahship. " 'We know this man,' they affirm, 'whence he is, but when the Christ cometh, no man knoweth whence he is.' Then said Jesus in the Temple as he taught, 'Ye do indeed know me and ye know whence I am,' " and then he goes on to point out a higher authorization for Messiahship than genealogical descent. Again, if Jesus had known of the Virgin Birth, he would not have been likely to refer to his mother's family and their home as his own kin and his own house;[9] and if Mary had known of his super-

---

[7] *Cf.* Westcott and Hort, and the Sinai-Syriac MS. *Cf.* an important discussion of early readings in Hastings' Bible Dictionary, Vol. II, pp. 644-645. Also Notes on Select Readings in Westcott and Hort's, The New Testament in the Original Greek.

[8] St. Matt. 13, 55. St. John 1, 45; 6, 42. St. Luke 4, 22.

[9] St. Mark 6, 4.

natural origin, it would have restrained her from joining his other friends, as she apparently did, on the occasion when they declared that he had gone mad.[10] Moreover, if any least hint of his virgin birth had ever come to their ears, the friends of Jesus would have been swift to advance it in support of their claim to an exalted position for their Master, while his enemies would at once have hastened to found on it a charge of scandal and shame.

Another significant item of evidence is the surprise Joseph and Mary showed at the announcement of the shepherds and at the outspoken blessing of Simeon.[11] The inference is plain that if they had so recently become aware of the uniqueness of their child, they could hardly have wondered at the homage paid him. Again, they are surprised and without understanding, when they find him at twelve years of age in the Temple, and he tells them that of course he must be about his father's business. Such surprise is only intelligible when we hear them saying to each other, "But his father is a carpenter!"

On the eighth day after the birth of Jesus he is taken to the Temple for circumcision and for the purification of his mother. But on the theory of the Virgin Birth there had been no legal uncleanness, and thus no ground for purification.

[10] St. Mark, 3, 31.21.
[11] St. Luke 1, 18-33.

The Biblical Evidence

Moreover, the narrator says it was "their" purification, though the Revised Version has changed the pronoun to "her" to accord with what was supposed to be proper.[12] In point of fact the Revisers were right and the narrator was mistaken in supposing that the father and the child were included in the ceremony, for according to the Levitical law it was the mother only who was unclean.[13] But his use of "their" indicates that, in the thought of the narrator, all who were concerned in the birth must be purified, and therefore Joseph as father must be included.

In order to legitimate any claim for Jesus to the title of Messiah it was necessary to show that he was a descendant from David, for all Jewish authorities were agreed that the Messiah could come of David's line only. The Christian advocates of Jesus' Messiahship therefore presented two genealogies to prove his Davidic descent.[14] These genealogies are based on a fanciful arrangement of generations and are in many respects different from each other. But they both agree in ending the chain of descent with Joseph. They would therefore have been useless if Joseph had not been in reality his father. The author or editor of the third Gospel has heard of the Virgin Birth, and while inclining to allow it, still

---

[12] St. Luke 2, 22.
[13] Lev. 12, 2.
[14] St. Matt. 1, 1-17; St. Luke 3, 23.

cannot bring himself to forego the advantage of a claim to Davidic descent which, however, could only be valid on the contrary supposition. He therefore inserts a clause of possible qualification, "as was supposed." But unless the supposition was correct, his genealogy was worthless. The endeavor not so much to examine what a passage says as to make it say what we think it ought to mean led the pious Annius of Viterbo at the close of the fifteenth century to suggest that this was not a genealogy of Joseph but of Mary. But this device must be rejected, first because there is no evidence that the Jews recognized the genealogies of women as constituting a legal right for their sons; and then because it would do the strongest violence also to the language of the passage, since it would require the meaning, being, as was supposed, the son of Joseph, but in reality the son of Mary, who was the daughter of Heli, who was the son of Matthat. It is probable, indeed, that Mary was not of the tribe of Judah, David's tribe, for she is said to have been a cousin or kinswoman of Elizabeth, who was of the tribe of Levi.[15] This view of Mary's descent finds confirmation in "The Testaments of the Twelve Patriarchs," a book dating probably not later than 135 A.D. Here the Messiah is said to be of the tribe of Levi, and again of the two tribes of Levi and

[15] Levi XV, iii, Sinker's Ed., p. 104.

Judah, as typical of his twofold office of priest and king.[16] The Epistle to the Hebrews reasserts that Jesus was of the tribe of Judah.[17] The author then goes on to point out the exalted position of Jesus, and this he does by declaring that his functions were like those of a half-mythical king of ancient Hebrew history, Melchizedek. But how much stronger would have been his demonstration if he had declared that the Holy Spirit was the immediate father of Jesus! Yet such a claim, superior as it would have been, he never mentions. He does assert that the exalted position of Jesus as the ideal priest in bringing men to God was not a matter of birth; he was "without father, without mother, without descent." He did not belong to an institutional order. His function was personal and individual, "having neither beginning of days nor end of life." This line of argument he would not have been likely to take if he had known of the Virgin Birth.

Another suggestion made to reconcile these genealogies with the Virgin Birth is that the genealogy of the husband may have been reckoned as that of the wife. But for this there is no shade of evidence, and it is directly disproved by the painful reform carried out under Ezra, in which Jews who had married foreigners were

[16] Heb. 7, 17; Rev. 1, 5.
[17] Heb. 7, 14.

compelled to divorce their wives and put away their children by them to prevent contamination of the holy race.[18] It is difficult to avoid the conclusion that to the compilers of these genealogies it was a matter of prime importance that Jesus should be by lineal descent a son of David and Abraham, and that his title to this could come only through Joseph. If Mary was of the tribe of Levi and if the birth of Jesus was not a natural one, he was not descended from David.

The Epistles of St. Paul, which are earlier in date than any of our Gospels, contain no mention of the Virgin Birth. St. Paul is of the same opinion as the genealogies of the Gospels, that Jesus was "made of the seed of David according to the flesh"; [19] and this is repeated in a later letter ascribed to him,[20] and again in the Epistle to the Hebrews.[21] St. Paul says, "God sent forth His Son, made of a woman, made under the law, to redeem them that were under the law." [22] The thought here is that a redeemer must be subject to like conditions with those whom he would redeem; he must be, as the apostle declares elsewhere, "the first-born among many brethren." [23] This thought he repeats in saying that

[18] Ezra 9 and 10.
[19] Rom. 1, 3.
[20] II Tim. 2, 8.
[21] Heb. 7, 14.
[22] Gal. 4, 4.
[23] Rom. 8, 29.

God sent His own Son "in the likeness of sinful flesh"; [24] an expression impossible of use by anyone who regarded the Holy Spirit as the immediate father of Jesus. Our earliest Gospel says that at Jesus' baptism he saw heaven opened and the Holy Spirit descending upon him and heard a voice saying to him, "Thou art my beloved Son, in whom I am well pleased." If this was the occasion when he became conscious of himself as in a special sense the son of God—and this seems indicated by the temptation which immediately followed—then he could have had no consciousness previously of a sonship conferred upon him by an exceptional method of birth, for these two ideas of sonship are opposed to each other. The latter is materialistic, implying that special sonship to God is conveyed by a physical process. In the thought of the former sonship is spiritual, consisting in likeness to God in character and not in a physical quality of blood. This other materialistic view of the divine element in Jesus effectually disqualifies him to be the Saviour of men; for that salvation depends, as St. Paul says, upon his being made of a woman, the first-born among many brethren, or, as the Epistle to the Hebrews has it, one who is touched with the feeling of our infirmities, being "in all points tempted like as we are, yet without sin." [25] But if a special

[24] Rom. 8, 3.
[25] Heb. 4, 15.

nature conveyed through a special method of generation rendered him immune to temptation, then every suffering human being might exclaim, "No comfort nor uplift for me can come from him; his nature shut him out from the conditions under which I live. His goodness was conveyed to him from without, but mine is not so conveyed to me. I must fight my battle, therefore, apart from him and alone." The doctrine of the Virgin Birth does thus in fact reduce Jesus to the status of an Arabian genie or a Greek demi-god, a being whom we can contemplate with wonder but with whom we can have no essential connection. But the whole soteriology of the New Testament rests upon the idea of the conquest of temptation, not its avoidance through an impossibility of yielding, due to a peculiar inheritance. This the author of the Epistle to the Hebrews emphasizes: "He that sanctifieth and they who are sanctified are all of one; for which cause he is not ashamed to call them brethren. . . . Forasmuch then as the childen are partakers of flesh and blood, he also himself likewise took part of the same, that through death he might destroy him that had the power of death . . . For verily he took not on him the nature of angels, but he took on him the seed of Abraham. Wherefore in all things it behooved him to be made like unto his brethren . . . For in that he himself hath suffered, being tempted, he is able to succour them that are

The Biblical Evidence

tempted."[26] Could there be a clearer statement of the essential oneness of Jesus with humanity?

To sum up our discussion thus far, we may say that there are two views in regard to the birth of Jesus, for each of which exegetical support may be found in the New Testament. One is that he had no human father but was born without human generation, his mother remaining after his birth as before, a virgin. This view is clearly asserted in one passage and perhaps asserted, probably at least implied, in another. These are the only references to this view in the Bible. One who holds it may therefore claim so much and no more Scriptural authority for his opinion. The other view is that Joseph was his father. This is directly asserted in one passage in the Authorized Version and in several of the early texts, and is implied in many passages of the New Testament. One who holds this view may therefore claim for it more extensive Scriptural authority. This is not the place to inquire whether the Greek manuscript text supporting both these views is a faithful transcript of the original document or whether changes by later editors are discoverable in it. That important question must be left for textual scholars to consider. It is sufficient for our purpose to recognize that both views find some support in early tradition, though it does not follow that the evidence is equally strong in both

[26] Heb. 2, 11 ff.

cases. The evidence on each side must be fairly weighed. It is, however, surprising that the incongruousness with their surroundings of the two passages supporting the former view should not have been more fully perceived by the authors or editors of our text, but that these two passages should be left almost isolated, like glacial boulders standing alone on a lowland plain.

If the objection is raised that we have been giving here too much consideration to the reasonableness of the situation, it may be well to refer the objector to the words of the judicious Richard Hooker: "Inasmuch as law doth stand upon reason, to allege reason serveth as well as to cite Scripture." [27]

[27] Eccles. Polity, Bk. II, Ch. V, p. 7.

CHAPTER II

THE GROWTH OF THE DOCTRINE

Though there is no contemporary evidence illustrating the steps by which the belief in the Virgin Birth attained its full growth, several tendencies of thought in the first two centuries may help to explain it. Justin refers to the fact that the supernatural birth of divinities was a common idea in the heathen world. Though it may appear strange to us that an advocate of the superiority of Christianity should think that this had any application to the case of Jesus, it would have seemed entirely natural to the Greek-speaking Christians of Asia that their religion should not lack this mark of authority which the religions about them possessed. That birth is possible by other means than ordinary generation was a very ancient belief, of which there are still survivals. Because it would be unscientific to attempt to prove a negative, all we can say is that such a birth may not be impossible. Just because, however, it was not the ordinary mode of human birth it would have seemed to ancient thought appropriate and necessary to a divine being; a remarkable being must have a remarkable origin. Another early belief, which came to be developed by Manes in the third century, declared that matter was essentially evil and therefore opposed to spirit. The world was consequently a dualism, a perpetual conflict between the material and the spiritual. This dualism largely influenced the Christian thought of the early centuries, though it was opposed by much of the Pauline theology and by the Johannine theology also. Through all the ages since, however, it has harmfully ravaged the popular conceptions of the relations of man and God—this idea that the human is the non-divine and the divine, the non-human. The more different then from the ordinary course of humanity anything is, the more likely, in this view, is it to be representative of the divine. This tendency would lead to easy acceptance of the supernormal element in the life of Jesus. Everything about him must be of the highest. His origin therefore must be free from all taint. Since the ordinary method of human generation was, in this view, unclean, demanding purification, his birth must have had no human father.

This demand would be strengthened by the growing conviction of his divine nature. Between the awed exclamation of Thomas, "My Lord and my God!" and the decree of Nicæa, there stretched three centuries of meditation on the nature of Christ, characterized by an award to him of more and more attributes belonging to the essential nature of God. The attributes selected varied with the problems forced upon the thought of different times, and the different attributions, as might be expected, under these circumstances, were not always consistent with one another. St. Paul, who credited Jesus with preexistence and regarded him as the embodiment of the eternal Son of God, would be likely to regard the story of the Virgin Birth as insignificant or suspicious; and for one who saw in him the Divine Logos an assertion of the Virgin Birth would be impossible. That which came to be accepted as the rounded-out Christian conception of Christ underwent a slow development, and this speaks for its genuineness. It would be strange if in the early stages of this development a mode of birth different from that of other beings had not been assigned to him. For as the idea gained ground that Jesus was the Son of God, it would become increasingly difficult to postpone to his baptism, in his thirtieth year, as does the second Gospel, his adoption as Son; he must have been God's chosen instrument from his birth, and therefore must have been plainly marked as such.

Still another influence tending to establish or strengthen the belief in a virgin birth was the growth of asceticism in early Christian society, with its conviction of the superiority of virginity to marriage. We see this depreciation of marriage already in the New Testament, as when St. Paul compares a wife and a virgin to the disadvantage of the former, and maintains that a father who gives his daughter in marriage does well, but one who gives her not does better. In his view, while marriage is entirely permissible to the Christian, abstention from marriage is more desirable.[1] That some upheld celibacy as the superior estate appears in the denunciation of them by a mid-century author. There are those, he says, who depart from the faith, "forbidding to marry," and he expressly directs the young women to marry and bring up children.[2] Again, praise, in the Vision of the Seer, is the lot of the 144,000 redeemed, who are men and virgins.[3] The tide of asceticism had not yet come to the full where it decreed celibacy essential to holiness, but the movement towards it was on the way. Now where marriage was so strongly felt to involve a taint or at least a status lower than the highest, the pious Christian would inevitably seek to remove the thought of such a taint from all connection with the Founder of his religion. Because everything else about Jesus was holy, his birth must have been holy, and therefore without human generation.

There are many persons who before they can

[1] I Cor. 7, 26 ff.
[2] I Tim. 4, 3; 5, 14.
[3] Rev. 14, 4.

The Growth of the Doctrine

bring themselves to consider the evidence in regard to the Virgin Birth, are perplexed by a previous question: How is it possible for the Bible to contain statements in conflict with one another? They have been accustomed to regard the Bible as one book presenting one outlook, one consistent system of doctrine, from beginning to end. Even when this has been superseded by the later view of the Bible as a literature, the conviction persists that all its parts bear witness to an underlying unity. And such is indeed the case. But the unity is not one of opinion or knowledge or outlook either upon the world or upon the conception of God. It is rather one of spiritual attitude, of upward look and reach, of increasing penetration into the depths of religious thought and loyalty to convictions attained. The ideas underlying these convictions may vary widely and antagonistically. For example, in the Jewish State, usury was forbidden; yet in the parable of the Householder and his Servants the servant is denounced as wicked for not having repaid his master with usury.[4] The primitive conception of the meeting-place of God with men was a garden; then a movable tent; then a gorgeous temple; while in the last book of the Bible it is a city, and this contains no temple, for the tabernacle of God is with men.[5] Jesus is con-

[4] *Cf.* Lev. 25, 37; Ps. 15, 5; St. Luke 19, 23.
[5] Gen. 2, 8; Exod. 25, 9; I Kings 6, 1; Rev. 21, 3.

tinually insisting on the changes which the law of development brings: "Ye have heard that it was said by them of old time. . . . But I say unto you." [6] Yet he is equally insistent in declaring that these changes are but such as are necessary to unite present practice with past precept and to reveal their underlying unity.[7]

The unity of the Bible is therefore in no way disturbed by varying or conflicting statements. In fact it would be an inaccurate and untrustworthy record of the relations of men and God in history if many of the earlier stages it narrates were not superseded by further and higher developments. We may consequently consider the conflicting evidence in regard to the Virgin Birth without feeling that we are in any way disloyal to our reverence for the Bible in recognizing in it divergent statements. St. Paul had apparently never heard of the Virgin Birth, for he is wholly silent in regard to it and his Christology has a totally different basis. What convinces him that Jesus is the Son of God is not any incident connected with his birth but his personal power, his holiness and his superiority to death.[8] If St. Paul did not regard the Virgin Birth as essential in Christianity, we need not so regard it. It is superfluous for us to be more orthodox than he.

[6] St. Matt. 5, 21-22.
[7] *Ibid.*, 5, 17-18.
[8] Rom. 1, 4.

We hold today to a sharp distinction between matter and spirit; but for the early Christian centuries this distinction did not exist. Spirit was a sublimated form of matter, the two passing into each other. Modern science is apparently tending in this direction again. The end towards which it is progressing seems to be the abolition of the distinction between mind and matter and the recognition of all matter as a form of force and force as a form of mind. Should this view become reasonably well established, we shall find ourselves living in what is literally a universe. The thought of the first century, therefore, saw no obstacle in the way of regarding the divinity of Christ as material, a substance implanted by non-human agency in the womb of the Virgin Mary. It was this non-human essence which made him *sui generis* different from other beings, a state which no other being could ever attain.

That is still to many persons today the basis of their conception of the divinity of Christ, a physical something implanted in him before birth which rendered him forever different from all other beings. And this much can be said for this view, that native endowment, that which differentiates one man from another, is ever a mystery. How far physical elements mingle with spiritual no one can tell. But that the physical is the determining, the characteristic element in personality, we cannot today believe. We must think that the will is the centre of personality, and that this rather than any material substance constitutes the person. We must regard the divinity of Christ therefore as consisting primarily in the unity of his will with the will of God. It was this which was the centre of his being; it was the completeness of this unity which constituted him unique, the fact that he could always and everywhere say, "Thy will be done." Such a sharing of the Divine will would give him access to others of the Divine powers; and we find him therefore possessed of knowledge of human character, of control over the minds and bodies of men and over natural forces, which so far transcend the powers of others that we sometimes calls them supernatural. But all these fell into the line of the development of personality around its centre, the will. Just as in the lower orders of creation the line between organic and inorganic is obscure, so the line between human and divine is difficult to draw; the one shades into the other. The human element in man shades into his divine element, and the divine in man shades into the divine in Christ, and the divinity of Christ shades into the divinity of God.

That there is thus a line running straight from man through Christ up to God is the master-key that unlocks the Christology of the New Testament. It contains, indeed, several systems of Christology, if we may use the word "system" where no one is developed with systematic exactness. The main objective, for example, of the Pauline theology can be reached along this line. It was necessary that one qualified to "condemn sin in the flesh" should be made "in the likeness of sinful flesh." [9] In order that those who were under the law might be redeemed, "God sent forth his Son, made of a woman, made under the law." [10] He is the "first-born among many brethren," [11] which could not be unless there were a nature common to both him and them. And this is emphasized more explicitly: "He that sanctifieth and they who are sanctified are all of one; for which cause he is not ashamed to call them brethren." [12] Consequently he is "touched with the feeling of our infirmities," since he "was in all points tempted like as we are, yet without sin." [13] It was a stage in the great line of spiritual evolution for God "in bringing many sons unto glory, to make the Captain of their salvation perfect through sufferings." [14]

It is but putting in different form the thought of the essential oneness of mind and matter to point out that modern science has abolished the distinction between differences of degree and of

[9] Rom. 8, 3.
[10] Gal. 4, 4.
[11] Rom. 8, 29.
[12] Heb. 2, 11.
[13] *Ibid.* 4, 15.
[14] *Ibid.* 2, 10.

kind. Heretofore a butterfly's wing was regarded as different in kind from a grain of sand; the two had nothing in common. But the butterfly's wing differs from the fin of a fish only in degree, because similar causes can be traced at work in the development of both. With a still wider outlook, we have come to recognize that all things are connected by an interlocking chain. The universe in all its parts has developed by successive stages from primæval germs, so that each part is related, closely or distantly, to every other part. We may not be able to detect all these different stages or degrees, but that they are there is a necessary part of our belief in the rationality of the universe. Just as a histologist can construct an unknown animal from a single bone, so, if we were wise enough, we could construct the world from a grain of sand. If we knew all in all of the flower in the crannied wall, we should know what God and what man is.

This does not mean that we are obliged to give up using the expressions, "differences in degree and in kind"; only it is to be remembered that they are not strictly accurate; they are loose and convenient modes of speech. It is in the main with the differences between objects that we are commonly concerned rather than with their unity. Yet while we rejoice in the glorious manifoldness of the world, it must never blind us to the fact of its profound, majestic, underlying unity.

The Growth of the Doctrine

This will recommend to us as all the more natural, all the more inevitable, the thought of which we were speaking, of a line from the lowest atom through man, through Christ, straight up to God. There are those who hesitate to allow this because of their desire to accent the difference between Christ Jesus and other beings. But such difference is quite as strongly insisted on by those who welcome the continuity of this line of ascent. Where the former, however, would be, at first at least, chary in allowing the existence of connecting links between Christ and lower beings, the latter would reverently welcome such links. It nevertheless would seem, that all should agree in recognizing the continuity of the chain when we reflect that it was precisely this which was asserted in the historic creeds which all respect. These creeds agree in maintaining both the divinity and the humanity of Christ. They felt the difficulty of combining the two because of their dualistic belief in the oppositeness of divine and human. Either one side was merged in the other, or the two were tied together and asserted as one without explanation. As long as dualism blocked the way the problem was insoluble. Only when it is recognized that humanity is divinity in germ and that divinity is humanity raised to the nth power, does a solution become possible. We may disagree with the Creeds of Nicæa and Chalcedon in their methods of explaining the unity of divine and human, but we fully agree with what they were endeavoring to assert—the likeness of Christ to humanitty and at one and the same time his difference from it.

The Virgin Birth is, therefore, in no way connected with the divinity of Jesus unless we regard that divinity as material. We may accept it or may reject it for a more spiritual idea of divinity, and in either case hold fast to the essential underlying truth of the differentness, the uniqueness, the majesty, the lordship of Christ, the eternal Son of God. We do not indeed venture to such a length as to say that Christ is God, for this would involve the inconceivable assertion that God Almighty was once born and died. Moreover, the Bible never declares, as a truth to be believed, that Christ is God. The awed, enthusiastic exclamation of Thomas when he is at last convinced of the reality of Jesus' resurrection, "My Lord and my God!" [15] is the only instance in the New Testament where the term "God" is directly applied to Christ, and this is the momentary utterance of excited emotion rather than a calm statement of rational opinion. The habit of founding doctrines solely upon Bible texts has been largely discontinued; but even granting them their legitimate authority, it is the consensus of different passages that constitutes this authority rather than isolated instances. For, as was said

[15] St. John 20, 28.

by the learned and pious Provost of King's College, Cambridge, Dr. Benjamin Whichcote, "No one institution depends upon one text of Scripture only. That institution which has but one text for it has never a one." [16]

I do not overlook the passages in the Book of Revelation in which Jesus is called the Alpha and Omega. "I am Alpha and Omega, the beginning and the ending, saith the Lord, which is and which was and which is to come, the Almighty." [17] But the one who here calls himself Alpha and Omega expressly disclaims worship, professing himself a fellow-servant with the Seer, and bids him worship God.[18] This inconsistency is altogether consistent with the usage of the author. "From him logical consistency in ideas and images and exclusiveness among them cannot be demanded. As he identifies Nero with one of the Beasts, and then immediately, unconsciously, and with no sign of transition, identifies him with the Beast as a whole, so here the highest angel and the beginning of the creation of God, the firstborn of every creature and the Prince of Heaven, the King of the new Kingdom and the Eternal Judge, pass naturally and unconsciously into one another. If this seems strange, it can be so only to one who comes expecting to find everywhere

[16] Aphorisms, 586.
[17] Rev. 1, 8-11.
[18] *Ibid.*, 22, 8.9.13.

the footprints of a carefully worked-out theological system, such as are those of the West. Such a system is not natural to the Oriental mind, and was foreign to the earliest days of Christianity. Valuable as such systems are, they are an adult growth, and in the history of Christianity it required several centuries and the influence of the West to produce them. Vision comes more naturally in the East than thought; and in a vision the images blend and pass into one another without condemning thereby the vision's genuineness or value.

"The point of view of the Seer then is continually changing. He conceives of Jesus now as the highest of the creatures, now as the Eternal beginning and end of all things. Our difficulty in comprehending this arises not only from the fact that to us each of these is a definite and separate conception, while to the author such definiteness and separation did not exist, but also from the single idea conveyed to us by the word 'angel' as compared with the double idea contained in the original, ἄγγελος. To the Greek this word meant not only one of those beings whom we call distinctively angels, but a messenger of any kind. To speak of Jesus as a divine ἄγγελος then in this primary sense of messenger would not be so foreign to the point of view which regarded him as Son of God as to speak of him as an 'angel.' Here again the Oriental mind, averse to minute distinctions, would probably have found no difficulty where the Western mind might readily find one." [19]

While then by no means refusing to allow to proof-text, miracle, or native physical endowment all the weight to which they are entitled, we may joyfully turn to a deeper ground for our belief in the divine Son of God, which we find summed up for us in the words of a distinguished modern theologian: "The crowning evidence of the divinity of Christ is that in yielding ourselves to him we find God." [20]

[19] Frederic Palmer: The Drama of the Apocalypse. The Macmillan Co., 1903, pp. 104, 105.
[20] Pres. Geo. E. Horr, D.D., Newton (Mass.) Theological Institution, Baccalaureate Sermon, June 3, 1923.

CHAPTER III

MIRACLES

Those who hold a materialistic view of the divinity of Christ sometimes suppose that the objection to its acceptance by others is due to a refusal to recognize the element of the supernatural. Yet so far is this from being the case that those who hold a more spiritual view object to the opposite opinion because it is not supernatural enough. They go further and consider it contrary to what they must regard as God's mode of action, for this they must believe to be ever rational and self-consistent. But if the Virgin Birth were something wholly unique, then the Divine action would be in this instance disjointed, unrelated to anything done by God before or after. It could therefore have no meaning, and having no meaning could not be part of that Word of God without which nothing was made which was made. Its isolation would make it non-natural rather than supernatural. If we allow dualism to come to our aid for a moment, we shall recognize nature, the state of things which is, having in it no self-directive force, inert and plastic, and alongside and above it the formative power of personality, moulding things after its will. This formative power which is above the natural order we may call supernatural. From this point of view our objection to the theory of the uniqueness of the birth of Christ is that it is not supernatural enough, that it does not accord with the universality, the rationality, the majesty, of God's mode of action. But after availing ourselves thus of the services of dualism we must reject it as a real interpreter and take the position that there are not two distinct realms but everywhere personality is dominant. We may indeed still use the terms "natural" and "supernatural," as we permitted ourselves to do with the terms "difference of degree" and "difference of kind," recognizing them as loose and inexact, serving as handy modes of thinking but often beclouding the reality.

This consideration of the supernatural will help us in meeting its sister-word "miracle." Those who accept the Virgin Birth regard it as a miracle; and they commonly assert, as we have said, that those who hold the opposite view do so because they disbelieve in miracles altogether. It may be well then to enter upon a somewhat extended digression to set forth our conception of the miraculous and show how fundamentally interwoven with Christianity we believe it to be.

Dualism long succeeded in imposing on Christian thought its dictum that a miracle was something contrary to natural law. Its voice was so successful in this respect that when modern science established the belief in the universality of law, this belief seemed to involve disbelief in Christianity because that was supposed to be tied to the dualistic view of miracles. Fifty years ago Matthew Arnold, who should have known better, could make the calm assertion with its air of settling the matter finally, "Miracles do not happen." It is safe today to reverse the assertion and say, miracles not only have happened but are happening. To deny the dualistic view of miracles a hundred years ago was to offer oneself as a target for the missiles "infidel" and "atheist." Then Christian thought began cautiously to whisper that after all the miracles were a heavy burden on Christianity. Today we have come to see in a miracle a material change dictated by mind. We are therefore affirming the entire normality of miracles and that a religion without them would be no religion. We do not believe in Jesus Christ because he worked miracles, but we could not believe in him if he had not worked miracles.

In applying this thought to the interpretation of miracles we shall confine our consideration of them to those mentioned in the New Testament; not because we would deny that the miracles mentioned elsewhere ever occurred, but because the former conform more plainly to our general law

Miracles 35

that a miracle is a material change dictated by mind.

The miracles of the New Testament may be divided into three classes—cases of healing, cases of raising the dead, and those which for lack of a better term we may call nature-miracles. The first class embraces nine-tenths of all the miracles narrated. The second class is mentioned in six narratives, three of which are manifestly of the same incident.[1] It is noteworthy that in this thrice told case Jesus expressly asserts that "the damsel is not dead, but sleepeth." Since in early Christian usage death was spoken of as a sleep and since the bystanders evidently regarded this as a case of genuine death, we will not dispute the common assumption that it was a case of death. There are then four cases of asserted raising of the dead, or if we include the resurrection of Jesus, five.[2] The nature-miracles include such as feeding of the thousands, the changing of water into wine, the walking on the water and the calming of the wind and the waves, possibly the

---

[1] St. Matt. 9, 18 f. St. Mark 5, 23 f. St. Luke 8, 41. St. Luke 7, 11 f. St. John 11, 43 f. Acts 9, 36 f.

[2] I do not include those mentioned in St. Matt. 24, 52.53. The fact that the graves were said to have been opened at the crucifixion but that the dead did not rise until after Jesus' resurrection, indicates that this was undoubtedly an addition by a later editor who wished his Master to appear as "the first-born of them that slept." The story occurs in only one Gospel, and that not the earliest. We might, however, include these cases in the second class mentioned above without detriment to the explanation offered in regard to them.

incidents narrated in the accounts of the barren fig tree, the money in the fish's mouth, the unusual haul of fish, and the Gadarene swine. It is plain that a key to the understanding of the miracles is to be sought in those of the first class.

It is only recently that the direct power of mind over matter has begun to be studied carefully, and we are already discovering that that power is much greater than had been supposed. It has, of course, long been known that one's beliefs and mental attitude have a profound influence on his body. Courage and cheer are potent factors in overcoming illness, and morale is as important to an army as guns. Many a soldier does not discover that he is wounded until after the excitement of battle has passed by. A further stage in the power of mind over matter is reached in the fact that the beliefs and attitude of one person—or to sum it all up in a word, his personality—may have a profound influence on the personality of another, and this not so much by argument and conviction as by impartation and absorption. The stronger nature gives itself to the weaker, which emerges from the contact with powers not before possessed. And—a step further still—these new powers are not confined to the mind but are operative also on the body of the recipient. The hypnotist says to his patient, "You cannot move your arm," and he cannot. The devout Catholic who kneels before the shrine at Lourdes, convinced of the healing power of the Blessed Virgin, rises and throws away his crutches. The revivalist says to the drunkard, "You are no more an outcast. Your craving for drink is gone," and behold! it is gone.

It will be remembered that we defined a miracle as a material change dictated by mind. It is plain then that in this impartation of personality in which resides the power to work miracles, we have what we may call the law of miracle. Those who maintain that a miracle is an event contrary to natural law will of course assert that a miracle can have no law. But, apart from our necessary belief that all things must have a rational basis, this declaration of independence in severing one miracle from another would make them each an anomaly. It may justly be objected, however, that our definition does not exclude the use by mind of means in realizing its dictation, and that if means are used, every result of human agency becomes a miracle. Strictly speaking, this is true. But we may legitimately conform to popular usage and apply the term "miracle" to those instances only in which the agency is direct or the means are unknown. It will of course follow that to those who see the means employed in realizing the dictated end the event will not be, in the popular sense, miraculous, while to those who do not see the effecting means the same event will be miraculous. An eclipse is not miraculous to an astronomer; to the wondering savages who watch his predictions come true it is a miracle.

It is in this principle or law of the impartation of personality that we may find an explanation of the first class of miracles which we mentioned—the works of healing. Here as elsewhere the measure of what can be given is conditioned by the capacity to receive. The higher personality cannot pour itself into the lower unless the lower contributes all the receptivity of which it is capable. The first condition for reception is willingness; and this implies a more or less complete conviction of the ability of the expected influx to accomplish the desired end. This necessary receptive attitude is called by Jesus belief, and its presence or absence conditioned the success or failure of his power to work miracles. On the one hand he declared "All things are possible to him that believeth," and on the other hand he could do no mighty works in a certain place because of their unbelief. We ourselves see this law in operation in comparatively simple cases. When we come into the presence of a strong noble nature, we are shamed out of our feebleness and ignoble motives and rise into high fellowship with it. Many cases of disease, such as nervousness, hysteria, headache, fever, abnormal appetites, divided personality, insanity, are cured completely or partially by the uprising response in the

Miracles 39

patient to a strong appealing personality. These are as truly instances of the law of miracle as were in their higher degree the mighty works of Jesus. "The works that I do," he declared, "shall ye do also." We have declared previously that we could not believe in him if he had not worked miracles. Not only his divinity but even his superiority in any degree to us would have been disproved if this great common law of miracle had not been superlatively operative in him.

But, it may be said, the miracles of healing reported of Jesus include a far greater range of disease than the kinds we have mentioned. This is true, and is precisely what is to be expected when we compare what may be called the size of his personality with ours. A personality greater in the nth degree will accomplish works greater in the nth degree also. But it is interesting to note that his power apparently did not extend to all cases. There is no record of a lacking limb replaced, nor, so far as we know, of the healing of an advanced case of tuberculosis or cancer. His power had, if we may so say, both its physical and spiritual limits.

But though we may trace this law through nine-tenths of the miracles attributed to him, yet we must pause, so it is thought, when we come to the second class of miracles mentioned—the raising of the dead, for nobody has ever seen one really dead restored to life. Perhaps this demand for a modern instance is begging the question. At all events, we may well consider whether experience does not furnish data enough to enable us to infer as possible the operation of the law of miracle in this field also. We ordinarily regard death and life as wholly different, with a sharp line between them. But those who have watched much over the dying have come to observe in many cases a certain zone or belt between this world and the next in which life and death are mingled. The dying man seems to be now in this present familiar world, now in a world different, more or less strange to us. Sometimes he professes to see those already gone and to talk with them, both of which experiences seem entirely natural to him. At times he is more dead and at times less dead, until the time comes when we say he is dead. But apparently a similarly mixed condition continues at first on the other side of death as well, and there is a zone there in which the spirit is living in both worlds. And just as when near the end here he communicated with those there, so when near the beginning there he may communicate by appearance or speech with those here. I say this without reference to the phenomena of so-called spiritualism, which imply a somewhat different psychology, and I am ready to grant that the reality of apparitions of the dead has perhaps not been indubitably demonstrated. But sufficient evidence exists to justify the claim that the hypothesis is not unreasonable.

Miracles

There seems, however, to be a time-limit. Evidence exists, which in my opinion is trustworthy, that the dead have appeared to the living within three or four days after death. I have never heard evidence of appearances after that time which seemed trustworthy. It is as if the spirit required a certain time to become adjusted to its new conditions, and during that period was still to some extent resident in its former zone.

Let it not be supposed that I am asserting these things as certain. We are here peering into a misty region where, like the half-blind man, we see men as trees walking. We are suggesting explanations which may be possible but which are not yet demonstrable. If, however, there is this zone we have described on each side of the line of death, it does not seem unreasonable to suppose that the efficient personality which could arrest death, such as we have seen to be operative in the first class of miracles, should be able in some cases to recall the spirit from the zone just beyond death. This would be to carry the operation of the law of miracle a step beyond cases of healing, but it would be a step in the same direction.

These considerations will throw light on the resurrection of Jesus. It would of course be inconceivable that so wonderful and mighty a personality could be overcome by death; he must have lived after it as truly as before. The only question that perplexes is as to his reappearance to his disciples. Apart from the Gospel testimony, the line of thought we have been pursuing would lead us to regard his reappearance as inherently probable. Using the thought to supplement the testimony of the Gospels, we can but regard his reappearance as established as fully as any event in his career. In view of the probability, which we have suggested, of the comparatively brief space of time within which reappearance after death is likely to take place, it seems probable that the date of his final disappearance was the third day after his death, as given in the third Gospel, rather than the prolonged time stated vaguely in round numbers in the later Book of the Acts as after "forty days." [3]

What became of his body is another question. But it is one which has for us only the interest of curiosity; it is in no way involved in the consideration of his reappearance. The genuineness of apparitions of those who have died may be questioned on many grounds, but in such judgment the disposition of their material bodies has never had weight. Whether the flesh and bones of Jesus were reanimated or not, how and when they finally disappeared, are matters of little interest and no significance. The important thing is that he, Jesus, was not held by death; his spirit after death took the same path our spirits must take. This is what is asserted in the clause of the

[3] *Cf.* St. Luke 24, 13.50 with Acts 1, 3.

Apostles' Creed, "He descended into hell," which has this meaning assigned to it in the rubric attached to the Creed in the Prayer Book of the Episcopal Church: "Any Churches may, instead of the words 'He descended into hell,' use the words 'He went into the place of departed spirits,' which are considered as words of the same meaning in the Creed." That the material body of Jesus rose through the clouds till it disappeared is not only inconceivable but it does not solve the problem of its final disposition. He, Jesus, was more than his body. It was the living Christ who was the inspiration of the early Church and who has continued to be the centre of Christianity ever since. The fate of his body is not of the least importance.

In regard to the second class of miracles then we may conclude that it seems probable that here too the law of miracle based on the impartation of personality is operative; and while this carries us a step beyond the preceding it is, we repeat, a step in the same direction.

In regard to the third class, the so-called nature-miracles, we have less experience of use for pointing to a possible explanation. We have, it is true, ever increasing instances of the conquest of nature by man, and it may be that some of these, such as radio and wireless telephony, may furnish the gate through which man may enter on a more direct control of nature. But at present we have little that helps us to understand some of these narratives, if taken at their face-value. Some of them, however, like the case of the barren fig-tree, seem almost patently not authentic; the original event, whatever it was, has been apparently colored for the purpose of edification. The attempt to explain the feeding of the thousands as an acted parable of the Last Supper is to many as unsatisfactory as is a literal interpretation of the event. The fact, however, that the authors narrate these miracles with entire seriousness, as matters of course, differing in no respect from other events which they regard as unquestioned, may lead us to respectful suspension of judgment with reference to them. They may point to unexplored regions in which forces reside yet unknown to us. We shall always be cautious in affirming what cannot be. Meantime, what we think of these miracles is of comparatively little importance, for they are few, they make no new contribution to our knowledge of Jesus, and their position in the gospel history is not fundamental. If we were asked, "How do you explain such and such a one?" perhaps our best answer would be, "I do not know." This answer, while asserting the right of suspended judgment, would leave untouched our belief in the great fundamentals of the gospel of Christ.

So far then from objecting to the Virgin Birth because it involves a miracle, our objection to it is, as we said, that it is not supernatural enough.

CHAPTER IV

THE VIRGIN BIRTH AND THE CREEDS

While the question of the Virgin Birth concerns all thoughtful minds, it has an especial interest for those who belong to a church in which such confessions of faith as the Apostles' and the Nicene Creeds are in use.[1] One who must at all costs be honest in his profession may ask himself, "Can I question the historicity of the Virgin Birth and still conscientiously repeat the Creeds?" His answer will depend to some extent upon the tone of his mind. If he is legally inclined, he will perhaps regard the Creed as like a contract in law, each of whose terms must have a fixed meaning, which must be assented to by every member of the Church using the Creed. Such a view is, however, untenable, for it stumbles at the very first words, "I believe in God the Father Almighty." But what is it to believe? To one person it is hardly more than to let a statement pass unchallenged. To another it is to give his

[1] It is noteworthy that in the longest and most complex of the three historic Creeds in the service of the Church—the Athanasian—and in the original form of the Nicene Creed, there is no mention of the Virgin Birth.

whole heart and soul and mind and strength to the truth affirmed. Is "God" a definite term, the same for every one? Does it not rather connote an almost infinite variety of ideas? "Father" may be a word of terror to the neglected waif of the streets, or it may be to the son of a good home a mirror of unspeakable loving-kindness. As soon as we have to do with creeds we enter a region where precision and community in exact understanding are impossible, for spiritual realities are not measured by the foot or the pound. The more determined the endeavor to secure such exactness, as in the Athanasian Creed and the Westminster Confession, the more complete has been the failure to attain a bond of union.

It is unwise then to regard a creed as a legal contract between an individual and the Church to which he belongs, or, to change the figure, as a central police-station which fixes authoritatively the meaning to be attached to its statements and prohibits all other meanings. To regard the Church's attitude to a creed as that of a custodian of an estate, whose duty is to preserve it and hand it on unchanged to coming generations, is to degrade both the Church and the creed, since for this no living custodian would be needed but a book would do as well. Such a guardian is like the Israelite who tried to keep his pot of manna beyond the allotted time, and who found that it became corrupt. There is many a man who stands clutching persistently the halter from which the horse has long ago escaped. If a creed is to be more than a scholastic treatise on theology, if it is to be a bond of union among believers, this bond must be found in the central thought underlying the creed rather than in its particular expressions. The framers of the creed expressed their thought in the form best fitted to the understanding of their time. But as times changed, this form became unintelligible, or expressive of an idea different from that originally intended, or one now seen to be not essential to that original thought or to be even detrimental to it. For example, no one now knows just what is meant by the phrase in the Apostles' Creed, "The communion of saints." Probably it originally meant participation in sacred things, such as the offerings and the sacraments; perhaps also the community of believers on earth with the saints and angels in heaven. Later ages, not understanding it, conceived it to mean the fellowship of the saints on earth, i.e. the Church. Scholars, however, assure us that whatever it means, this it cannot mean, but just what it does mean and why it was included in the Creed they do not know.[2]

Again, there are many today who are silent when they come to the phrase, "I believe in the resurrection of the body," for probably no one holds that his present body will stand up living

[2] *Cf.* A. C. McGiffert: The Apostles' Creed, p. 200 *f.*

after death. But this article was intended to be a confession of belief in the preservation of personal identity. To the framers of the article, the idea of personal existence apart from a body was inconceivable, or if conceivable, pagan. Therefore they dressed their belief in clothes which seemed to them proper and essential. But while we hold the belief as strongly as they did, the clothes have become impossible for us. It is no diminution of belief then, it is its fulfilment, when we translate this article to mean the preservation of personal identity.

"Then," one may say, "would it not be better to translate the whole Creed into the language and thought of today, so that we may mean exactly what we say?" Yes, undoubtedly it is desirable that each one should do this for himself. But the moment we regard our translation as the final standard for the present or the future, we are digging the same pit for others which our forefathers dug for us. For if a creed is not to become a fossil, it must be continually translated into the differing thought of each new age. In doing this it will of course be necessary to be governed by loyalty to what was the original intention of the framers of the creed. Every scholar or reformer has a right to point out fresh meanings, provided they are in the interest of the creed's original intention—are larger, less contradictory, more spiritual, more indicative of the

The Virgin Birth and the Creeds 49

symbol's real signification. We are not changing a creed when we are freeing it from its own inconsistencies and giving more unhampered and fuller life to the ideas which constituted its value. For that which enables the essential self of a thought to rise to greater completeness and acquire a larger hold on men, is helping it to become more fully its real self; and the name for that process is not decay but development. If we refuse to recognize the legitimacy of such interpretation, we condemn our Lord. For he took words which had a definite meaning for the churchmen of his day—"righteousness," "kingdom," "Messiah"—and gave them meanings which were wholly different. This created uncertainty and disturbance. "How long wilt thou make us to doubt? If thou be the Christ, tell us plainly." He was even charged with destroying religion; but he declared he was fulfilling it. The Epistle to the Hebrews is an elaborate attempt to give to the whole Jewish priestly and sacrificial system a meaning flatly in opposition to the popular one and directly non-Jewish. Yet the ages have justified such a course as the only one possible if the present at any stage is to be grafted on the past. To refuse such translation or spiritualization is to compel each generation to make a sharp break with the past and start housekeeping without any furniture. Instead of declaring that fixity of interpretation is of the essence of a creed, it would be more accurate to say that continual reinterpretation is essential to a creed. Creeds are guide-posts. Now the guide-posts do not determine the road, but the road determines the guide-posts.

Christian faith is the same in its essence in every age, and to assert this unity is the object of a creed. But this unity is one of aim and spirit rather than of intellectual content. Instead, therefore, of dispensing with the historic creeds and making new ones every few years, greater unity is secured by preserving the original symbols with free interpretation and loyalty to their aim and spirit. An algebraic formula is true in every age because its terms are applicable under all conditions. So a theologic symbol—for such was the original name for a creed—may serve the important function of emphasizing unity with the past, provided interpretation of its terms is combined with loyalty to its spirit. This is not to concede that intellectual opinions in religion are of no importance. They are of much importance, but their importance is distinctly secondary to rightness of spirit and aim, for this is the very essence of the union of the soul with God and of man with his fellow-believers. Above all, however erroneous opinions may be and however contrary to any given orthodoxy, they do not necessarily constitute heresy, for heresy is by no means the same as error. Error is the holding of an opinion which is not true. But heresy is the holding of such an opinion from an evil motive—some disinclination to recognize the truth, some unwillingness to change one's course, some personal dislike or spite towards those who hold an opposite opinion. For the root of heresy is self-assertion. Just as faith is the yielding of one's self wholly to what is representative of God, so its opposite, heresy, is the putting of one's preference in between the truth and one's self; and so, even an opinion in itself true may become heretical if held viciously. We may be in error through no fault of our own, but heretics we cannot be unless to our intellectual error we join some moral evil. It is for this reason that St. Paul classes heresy among the works of the flesh: "Now the works of the flesh are manifest, which are these: adultery, uncleanness, idolatry, hatred, wrath, heresies, envyings, drunkenness, and such like."[3] That is the class in which it belongs, for there is always a self-indulgent element in it. It is a sin one can never fall into who is pure of life and eager for the truth. Bishop Jeremy Taylor says, "No man is a heretic against his will. . . . If a man mingle not a vice with his opinion, if he be innocent in his life, although deceived in his doctrine, his error is his misery, not his crime. . . . A wicked person in his error becomes heretic, when a good man in the same error shall have

[3] Gal. 5, 20.

all the rewards of faith. For whatever an ill man believes, if he therefore believe it because it serves his own ends, be his belief true or false, the man hath an heretical mind; for to serve his own ends his mind is prepared to believe a lie. But a good man that believes what, according to his light and upon the use of his moral industry, he thinks true, whether he hits upon the right or no, because he hath a mind desirous of truth and prepared to believe every truth, is therefore acceptable to God; because nothing hindered him from it but what he could not help—his misery and weakness; which being imperfections merely natural, which God never punishes, he stands fair for a blessing of his morality, which God always accepts." [4]

The article in the Apostles' Creed on the Virgin Birth was intended, if we may trust historical investigation, not primarily to assert the unusualness of the birth of Jesus but rather his historic reality. It was levelled against the Docetism which declared that he was not a real being but was human only in appearance. In opposition to this view the Creed asserts that he had a real date in history, a real birth and death, and it points to his humanity emerging from the grave and merging with divinity. One who holds these fundamental truths may therefore claim the right to use the Creed, even if he rejects the theory of a

[4] Liberty of Prophesying, Sec. 12, 8, 22.

non-human birth in the case of Jesus; for it is unity with the spirit of a creed rather than with its intellectual content which conveys a right to its use. It is not wise to stake on a detail of history, confusedly stated and unverifiable, the blessings which come from loving worship of Christ the Lord, and to warn men that they cannot have the latter without the former. Our Lord himself never referred to the manner of his birth; and to erect into an essential of his religion something he never mentioned is to make Christianity more orthodox than Christ.

The fact that we are wisely illogical often saves us from the harm in erroneous doctrines. Probably no sternest Calvinist or Catholic ever realized fully what he professed to believe of the damnation of unbaptized infants. So there are many who hold the Virgin Birth who through lack of full consideration escape its pernicious consequences. Apart from the fact that ecclesiastical authorities often make it a shibboleth of religion and endeavor to exclude from the Christian ministry those who do not hold it, it is derogatory to the truest view of the union of the sexes. This union on its physical side it declares to be impure. Instead of seeing in it the pure and lofty sacrament of love, it brands it as something in which a divine being could have no part, and thereby stigmatizes an essential and God-ordained act as unworthy of God. The noblest instincts of love have indeed surmounted this pernicious teaching and sanctified all aspects of wedded union. But this has been done, not with the aid of the Virgin Birth, but in spite of it. This degradation finds no warrant in word or act of Jesus. For he ever exalted fatherhood. "Father" was to Him a sacred word, the highest and most significant he could use in interpreting the relations between God and man. This he could not have done if there was to his mind in the relationship something inherently dishonoring to the highest ideal. That entire freedom from taint which the Virgin Birth ascribes to Jesus rightly, but seeks to guarantee in a manner different from what was in reality the case, this must be possible for every one born of woman: "Else," as St. Paul in another connection says, "else were your children unclean, but now are they holy." [5]

In what has been here said of the Virgin Birth we have endeavored to distinguish between its possibility and its historicity. Its possibility we have not denied; for there is at present by no means sufficient scientific knowledge to warrant us in declaring what is impossible, except with the qualification, "so far as we know." As to its historicity we have endeavored to present judicially the evidence, so that every intelligent and impartial student may weigh both sides. But we

[5] I Cor. 7, 14.

must insist that it is a detail of Christian tradition of no importance whatever to the Christian religion, and that an opinion either way should have no effect upon any man's religious or ecclesiastical standing. If one is frivolous or godless, he is a genuine Pauline heretic, no matter what opinion of the Virgin Birth he may hold. But if the fatherhood of God, the divinity of Christ, and the glory of immortality are vital realities with him; if they are the steering forces of his life and the spring of his work; if men take knowledge of him that he has indeed been with Jesus; then we shall be unwise to attempt to silence him, no matter in what intellectual terms he may interpret these great realities. To exclude one who exultingly holds the divine Lordship of his dear Master Christ and his Master's triumphant rising from the dead because he cannot explain the mode of Jesus' birth or his resurrection, is to erect barriers ourselves where Christ put none. The *articulus stantis vel cadentis* of the Church is not orthodoxy, important as that is, but holiness. To cast out a man who is holy because he is not orthodox, is like hunting for a gas-leak with an open lamp; success can only bring disaster. The shock to the community at seeing the spirit of Christ officially disowned is more harmful to religion than any intellectual errors which might spring from his teaching. The Protestant Episcopal Church not only bids her members to hold the faith but she wisely teaches them how to hold it. Not in unity of opinion, in the bond of a common creed, or in rightness of belief; these may all be valuable, but yet she shows unto us a more excellent way. We are to hold the faith in unity of spirit, in the bond of peace, and in righteousness of life.

Those were wise words which were uttered by Dr. Charles Gore, formerly Bishop of Oxford, in which he pleads for what he calls, "the special vocation of the scholar" as necessary to preserve the life of the Church. "This vocation," he says, "lies in great part in purging the current tradition or enlarging it by perpetual recurrence to the divine originals. Thus the real security of a Church, as against the common tendency to doctrinal deterioration, lies in giving free scope to this, the scholar's gift of knowledge. And the requirement which this lays upon the ordinary members of the Church is that they should be ready to mortify the desire (so natural to human laziness) to be exempted from the moral and spiritual trouble involved in relearning old truths in a completer or purer form, and so taking their part in 'testing all things and holding fast that which is good.' " [6]

[6] Address by Bishop Gore, quoted in *The Churchman,* March 17, 1906, p. 411.

www.ingramcontent.com/pod-product-compliance
Lightning Source LLC
Chambersburg PA
CBHW072016060426
42446CB00043B/2571